VERMONT FAVORITES

Compiled by Ellen Doon

A Collection of Favorite Vermont Recipes

THE NEW ENGLAND PRESS, INC.

For additional copies write to:
The New England Press
P.O. Box 575
Shelburne, Vermont 05482

Lettered and illustrated by Jan Siegrist

ISBN 0-933050-94-1

PRINTED IN THE UNITED STATES OF AMERICA

CONTENTS

Breads

Desserts

And Furthermore

INTRODUCTION

When the first settlers came to Vermont, they brought with them much of England, not the least of which was its style of cooking. Traditional Vermont cooking is therefore British at its core, but it has been greatly modified and enhanced by the creative use of local ingredients. Other cuisines also influenced Vermont cooks, especially that of Vermont's northern neighbors, the French Canadians. This book is a collection of favorite recipes that have been prepared Vermont's own way and enjoyed by Vermonters for generations.

The early settlers found all they needed for an ample living in Vermont. The forests teemed with deer and other game, and the lakes and streams were filled with trout. Once the rocky fields were cleared, they yielded abundant crops of corn and wheat. Gardens, too, flourished despite the short growing season, and produced large quantities of onions, tomatoes, beans, pumpkins, and other vegetables. Because of early frosts, vegetables such as tomatoes had to be picked before they ripened, but they never went to waste. In addition to cultivated food, Vermonters have always enjoyed the many palatable treasures that grow wild in the state's woods and meadows. The gathering seasons for blackberries, dandelions, butternuts, and delicate fiddlehead ferns are still eagerly awaited each year.

Apples thrive in the Green Mountain State and are an important part of Vermont cooking. Thousands of bushels of the McIntosh variety are picked each fall and baked into pies and muffins, just eaten on their own, or pressed into cider. Apple cider is a great favorite; hot mulled cider is the perfect drink for a chilly autumn evening.

The same trees which, in the fall, turn the

Green Mountains crimson and gold, produce in the spring one of the most important and best-loved ingredients in Vermont recipes. Maple syrup and sugar are staples in Vermont cooking. The first settlers learned what they later called "sugaring off" from the Native Americans, who had been cooking with maple for hundreds of years. When the warm days and cold nights of early spring cause the sap of the maple tree to run, spouts are driven into the bark, and buckets are hung from them to catch the sap. The sap is then collected and boiled down into sweet, thick syrup and hard sugar crystals. Years ago, maple syrup and sugar were often substituted for expensive white sugar and other sweeteners because they were cheaper, more readily available, and, in the opinion of most Vermonters, made things taste better.

Pork was the backbone of the Vermont diet in the old days. Pigs were easy to raise and made very good eating. The meat was preserved in brine and stored by most households in barrels in the cellar. Inventive Vermont cooks kept a steady diet of pork from becoming boring by serving it in everything from main dishes to desserts. Pork Apple Pie is but one delicious example of this imaginative use of pork.

Vermont is ideal for dairy farming and dairy products are a staple in Vermont cooking. Cheese and sweet cream are used liberally in many different dishes. Sour milk and sour cream, too, are an integral part of Vermont's cuisine. In the days before refrigeration and pasteurization, milk and cream soured quickly. Rather than wasting them, Vermont cooks found ways to use them, and in so doing improved many already good recipes and created some wonderful new ones.

The typical Yankee frugality demonstrated

by Vermonters as they substituted available ingredients and created delectable dishes from sour cream and green tomatoes was an important force in shaping Vermont cooking, as was the inventiveness of the Vermont cooks who adapted their cooking style to new kinds of food in a new region. Before long the substituted ingredients became the preferred ones, and these delicious new recipes quickly became favorites which still endure.

Blackberry Cordial

3 quarts fresh blackberries
2/3 cup water
1 3/4 cups sugar
2 teaspoons whole cloves
1/2 stick cinnamon
1/2 tablespoon nutmeg
1 pint brandy

Crush the berries in a large pot; add the water. Cook, but do not boil, until the berries are soft and their juices are released. Strain the berries through cheesecloth. Return 1 quart of the juice to the pot. Add the sugar, cloves, cinnamon, and nutmeg. Boil for 15 minutes. Strain to remove the cinnamon stick and cloves. Cool completely. Add the brandy; pour the cordial into a clean, open-mouthed jar and cover. Let stand for 1 month before using, then store in a sterilized bottle. Makes about 1 1/2 quarts.

Mulled Cider

½ gallon apple cider
½ teaspoon whole cloves
¼ cup brown sugar
¼ cup maple syrup
3 sticks cinnamon
Extra cinnamon sticks for garnish (optional)

Combine all of the ingredients (except the garnish) in a large pot; bring to a boil. Reduce the heat and simmer for 5 minutes. Strain to remove the cinnamon sticks and cloves. Serve hot with half of a fresh cinnamon stick in each cup, if desired. Makes about 2 quarts.

Raspberry Shrub

3 quarts fresh raspberries
1 quart white vinegar
8-10 cups sugar, approximately

Place the raspberries in a large bowl; cover with the vinegar. Let stand for 24 hours. Strain through cheesecloth into a large saucepan. Add 4 cups of sugar for each quart of juice. Boil the mixture until it is a thick syrup, 15-20 minutes. Cool, then store in sterilized bottles. Makes about 2 quarts of shrub.

Mix 1 part shrub with 3 parts ice water to serve by the glass or by the pitcher.

Chicken in Cream

3-4 medium boneless, skinless chicken breasts
3 tablespoons all-purpose flour
4 tablespoons butter
Salt and pepper
1 small onion, finely diced
$\frac{1}{4}$ teaspoon ground cloves
2 cups heavy cream

Cut the chicken into 2-inch pieces; roll in the flour. In a large skillet, melt the butter. Add the chicken and lightly brown. Place the chicken in a baking dish; salt and pepper to taste. Heat the onion, cloves, and cream in the butter remaining in the skillet until hot; pour over the chicken. Cover tightly; bake in a preheated 300°F oven for 1 hour. Remove the chicken pieces to a serving dish. Pour a little of the cream sauce over top. Serve the remaining sauce in a gravy boat or bowl. Serves 4.

Chicken Pot Pie

1 chicken (4-5 pounds), cut up
1 medium onion, chopped
3 large carrots, chopped
2 stalks celery, chopped
3 large potatoes, diced
½ teaspoon dried rosemary
½ teaspoon dried thyme
½ teaspoon dried sage
1 chicken bouillon cube
1 teaspoon salt
1 teaspoon pepper
2 tablespoons butter
½ cup all-purpose flour
½ cup water
1 recipe pie pastry for 2 crusts

Place the chicken, onion, carrots, celery, potatoes, rosemary, thyme, sage, bouillon cube, salt, and pepper in a large pot. Add enough water to cover; bring to a boil. Reduce heat. Simmer, covered, until the meat is tender and ready to come off the bone, about

1½ hours. Remove the chicken; strain the vegetables, reserving 2 cups of the broth. When the chicken is cool enough to handle, remove the meat from the bones; cut into 2-inch pieces. Discard the bones and skin. In a large saucepan, melt the butter; add the 2 cups reserved chicken broth. In a separate bowl, combine the flour and water to make a paste. Add the flour paste to the chicken broth mixture; cook until smooth, stirring constantly. Add the chicken and the vegetables. Pour into a deep pie shell and cover with top crust. Pinch edges of the pastry together and cut slits in the top to vent. Bake in a preheated 400°F oven for 30 minutes or until browned. Serves 6.

Maple Baked Ham

1 ham
1 cup maple syrup per 5 pounds ham
3-4 tablespoons all-purpose flour

To bake the ham, remove the skin; place in a shallow pan. Bake in a preheated 325°F oven. It is done when it reaches 150°-155°F on a meat thermometer, about 20 minutes per pound. When HALF done, remove half the drippings and set aside. Pour the maple syrup over the ham; baste every 20 minutes until done. Remove from the oven. Pour off the maple-flavored drippings into a saucepan. Add the drippings previously set aside and heat. Thicken with the flour; serve as a sauce.

Cider Baked Ham: Bake ham as above, only substitute 1½ quarts cider for the maple syrup; add ¼ teaspoon ground cloves to the drippings as you make the sauce.

Tomato Rarebit

½ pound sharp cheddar cheese
1 can (10¾ ounces) condensed tomato soup
1 soup can water
1 teaspoon sugar
1 teaspoon Worcestershire sauce
2 tablespoons all-purpose flour
2 tablespoons water
8 or more slices of bread, toasted

Shred the cheese. In the top of a double boiler, combine the cheese, tomato soup, soup can of water, sugar, and Worcestershire sauce. Heat until the cheese is melted and the mixture is very hot, stirring frequently. In a small bowl, make a paste with the flour and 2 tablespoons water; add to the cheese mixture and stir. Serve over the toast. Serves 4.

Tourtière (Pork Pie)

1 pound ground pork
1 pound ground beef
1 large onion, chopped
1 boiled potato, diced
1 ½ teaspoons salt
1 teaspoon pepper
½ teaspoon ground cloves
2 cups bread crumbs
1 recipe pie pastry for 2 crusts

Brown the pork, beef, and onion together in a skillet. Drain off any excess fat. Remove the mixture to a large bowl. Add the potato, salt, pepper, cloves, and bread crumbs; mix well. Roll out half of the pastry to form a bottom crust and place in a 10-inch pie pan. Fill with the meat mixture. Roll out the remaining pastry; place on top of the meat. Pinch the edges of the pastry together. Cut slits in the top to vent. Bake in a preheated 425°F oven for 30 minutes. Serve warm. Serves 6-8.

Trout in Cream

2 trout, ½ - ¾ pounds each
3 tablespoons all-purpose flour
⅓ cup butter
1 small onion, diced
⅔ cup heavy cream
Salt and pepper

Clean and wash the fish well, leaving on the heads and tails to prevent the trout from falling apart while cooking. Roll them in the flour. In a large skillet, melt half of the butter. Add the fish and brown on both sides. Salt and pepper to taste; cover. Cook for 6-8 minutes. Remove the trout from the pan and keep hot in a serving dish. Brown the onion slightly in the remaining butter; add the cream and heat, but do not boil. Pour over the trout. Serves 4.

Venison Roast

5 pound venison roast
3 tablespoons butter
Several wide slices fat bacon or salt pork
7 medium carrots
3 large onions
2 medium turnips
2 stalks celery
2 teaspoons parsley flakes
¼ teaspoon dried thyme
1 cup port or white wine
2 cups boiling water
5 large potatoes
Salt and pepper
2 tablespoons all-purpose flour
2 tablespoons water

In a deep baking pan, brown the roast on all sides in the butter. Cover the top of the roast well with wide strips of fat bacon or salt pork. Coarsely chop the carrots, onions, turnips, and celery; add to the pan with the parsley, thyme, wine, and boiling water. Cover;

cook in a preheated 300°F oven for 3-4 hours. When half done, quarter the potatoes and add to the pan. Salt and pepper the roast to taste. Add more water and wine in the original proportion if too much of the liquid has evaporated in cooking.

When done, remove the bacon or salt pork; arrange the meat and vegetables on a large serving platter. Combine the flour and 2 tablespoons water in a small bowl and add to the liquid in the pan. Serve as gravy. Serves 8.

Vermont Baked Beans

2 cups yellow-eyed beans (navy or pea beans may be substituted)
½ teaspoon baking soda
½ cup maple syrup
¼ cup chopped onion
1 tablespoon prepared mustard
2 tablespoons ketchup
⅓ cup brown sugar
3-4 strips fat bacon

In a large pot, soak the beans overnight in the baking soda and enough water to cover. In the morning, pour off the water; add fresh water to cover. Bring to a boil. Reduce the heat; simmer until the beans are tender and their skins flake off easily when you blow on them, 30-35 minutes. Drain the beans; place in a baking dish. Add the maple syrup, onion, mustard, ketchup, and brown sugar; mix well. If the beans are not covered, add enough water to cover. Lay the bacon strips across the top of the beans; cover. Bake in a preheated 300°F oven for 3-4 hours. Serves 4.

Cheese and Cabbage Potatoes

4-5 medium potatoes, quartered
1 medium head cabbage, finely chopped
1 stalk celery, finely chopped
½ teaspoon parsley flakes
¼ pound sharp cheddar cheese, shredded
1 cup light cream
Salt and pepper

Place the potatoes, cabbage, and celery in a large pot; sprinkle with the parsley. Add water just to cover; simmer, covered, for about 20 minutes, or until the potatoes are tender. In a small saucepan, combine the cheese and cream; heat just until the cheese is melted, but do not boil. Keep hot until the vegetables are done. Remove the vegetables to a serving platter; salt and pepper to taste. Pour the cheese sauce over top. Serves 6.

Corn Chowder

4 medium potatoes, diced
2 medium onions, finely chopped
1 stalk celery, finely chopped
1 tablespoon butter
2 cups whole kernel corn
1 medium carrot, diced
1 quart milk
3 tablespoons all-purpose flour
Salt and pepper

In a large saucepan, lightly brown the potatoes, onions, and celery in the butter. Add the corn, carrots, and 3½ cups of the milk; simmer until the potatoes are tender. In a small bowl, combine the flour and remaining ½ cup milk; stir. Add to the chowder. Continue cooking and stirring until the chowder thickens to desired consistency. Add more milk, if too thick; add more flour-and-milk, if too thin. Salt and pepper to taste. Serves 4.

Dandelion Greens

1½ pounds dandelion greens
¼ pound salt pork
2 tablespoons butter
Salt and pepper

Wash the greens thoroughly; cover with water in a large saucepan or large pot. Boil rapidly for 10 minutes. Drain; add the salt pork. Cover with fresh water; bring to a boil again. Reduce the heat; simmer for 1½ hours. Drain; remove to a serving bowl. Add the butter; toss lightly to mix throughout the greens. Salt and pepper to taste. Serves 4.

Fried Green Tomatoes

4-6 green tomatoes
$\frac{1}{4}$ cup all-purpose flour
Salt and pepper
Bacon fat for frying

Thinly slice the tomatoes and dredge the slices in the flour. Salt and pepper to taste. In a large skillet, fry the tomatoes in the fat for 8-10 minutes or until browned. Serves 4-6, depending on the size and number of tomatoes used.

Cream of Fiddlehead Soup

4 chicken bouillon cubes
4½ cups boiling water
3 tablespoons butter
1 medium onion, finely chopped
4 tablespoons all-purpose flour
2 cups fiddlehead greens
1 cup light cream
Salt and pepper

In a large saucepan, add the bouillon cubes to the boiling water; stir and set aside. In a separate large saucepan, melt the butter. Sauté the onion in the butter, but do not brown. Add the bouillon broth; gradually add the flour. Bring to a boil, stirring constantly. Add the fiddlehead greens; cover. Simmer for 15-20 minutes. Add the cream and salt and pepper to taste. Heat, but do not boil. Serves 4.

Fiddlehead greens are gathered in the spring. Look for them fresh in grocery or gourmet food stores in early May; they can be found canned or frozen during the rest of the year.

Creamed Onions

3 jars (12 ounces each) small, boiled onions; or 3 large onions, peeled, boiled, and coarsely chopped

3 tablespoons butter

½ cup grated mild cheddar cheese

1 tablespoon all-purpose flour

1 cup milk

Salt and pepper

Place the onions in the bottom of a shallow baking dish or pie pan. Dot with the butter; sprinkle the cheese evenly over the onions. In a small bowl, stir the flour into the milk; pour over all. Salt and pepper to taste. Bake in a preheated 350°F oven for 20-25 minutes. Serves 4-6.

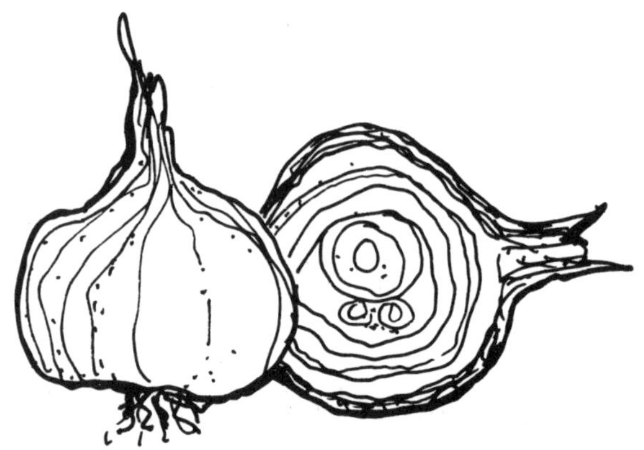

Johnnycake

1 teaspoon baking soda
2 cups sour milk or buttermilk
¾ cup all-purpose flour
2 ⅓ cups cornmeal
½ teaspoon salt
½ teaspoon baking powder
¾ cup sugar
2 eggs, beaten
2 tablespoons butter, softened

Dissolve the baking soda in the sour milk or buttermilk. In a large bowl, mix together the flour, cornmeal, salt, and baking powder. In a separate bowl, combine the sugar, eggs, and butter. Gradually add the flour mixture to the sugar mixture. Add the sour milk or buttermilk; mix well. Pour the batter into a greased 9-inch square pan. Bake in a preheated 400°F oven for 30-35 minutes. Serves 6.

Pumpkin Bread

2 cups cooked pumpkin, mashed well
4 eggs, beaten
¾ cup vegetable oil
½ cup water
4 cups all-purpose flour
1 teaspoon salt
3 cups sugar
2 teaspoons baking soda
1 teaspoon cinnamon
½ teaspoon nutmeg
½ teaspoon ginger

In a medium-size bowl, mix the pumpkin with the eggs, oil, and water. In a large bowl, sift together the flour, salt, sugar, baking soda, cinnamon, nutmeg, and ginger. Gradually add the flour mixture to the pumpkin mixture; mix thoroughly. Pour into 2 greased 8½x4½-inch loaf pans. Bake in a preheated 375°F oven for 40-45 minutes, or until a wooden pick inserted near the center of each loaf comes out clean. Makes 2 loaves.

Vermont Oatmeal Bread

2 cups rolled oats
2 cups boiling water
1 tablespoon shortening
⅔ cup maple syrup
1 teaspoon salt
1 package active dry yeast
½ cup warm water
5 cups all-purpose flour

In a large bowl, pour the boiling water over the oats. Stir in the shortening, maple syrup, and salt; let stand until lukewarm. In a separate bowl, dissolve the yeast in the warm water; add to the oat mixture. Gradually stir in the flour; the dough will become quite stiff. Turn onto a lightly floured surface and knead well. Shape into a ball and place in a greased bowl. Cover; let rise in a warm place until doubled, about 1 hour. Punch the dough down; divide in half and form 2 loaves. Place each in a greased 9x5x3-inch loaf pan. Cover; let rise in a warm place until doubled, about 1 hour. Bake in a preheated 375°F oven for 1 hour. Makes 2 loaves.

Sour Cream Biscuits

1 teaspoon salt
1 teaspoon baking soda
1 teaspoon baking powder
2 cups all-purpose flour
1 cup sour cream
$\frac{1}{4}$ cup milk

In a large bowl, sift together the salt, baking soda, baking powder, and flour. Gradually add the sour cream, mixing well to form a soft dough. On a lightly floured surface, roll out the dough to a $\frac{1}{2}$-inch thickness. Cut with a floured round cookie cutter or drinking glass. Place the biscuits on a greased baking sheet; brush the tops lightly with the milk. Bake in a preheated 400°F oven for 20 minutes or until golden brown. Makes 12-15 biscuits.

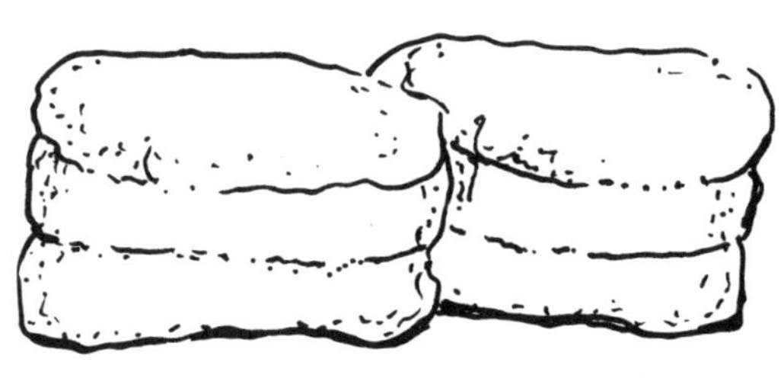

Blackberry Pie

¼ cup all-purpose flour
½ cup maple sugar
½ cup sugar
⅛ teaspoon salt
3 cups fresh blackberries
1 recipe pie pastry for 2 crusts
¼ cup cold water
2 tablespoons butter

In a large bowl, sift together the flour, maple sugar, sugar, and salt. Add the berries; mix well. Roll out half the dough to form a bottom crust and place in a 9-inch pie pan. Turn the berry mixture into the pie shell. Pour the water over all; dot with the butter. Roll out the remaining pastry; place on top of the berries. Pinch the edges of the pastry together; cut slits in the top to vent. Bake in a preheated 450°F oven for 10 minutes. Reduce the heat to 350°F; continue baking for 30 minutes. Cool before serving. Serves 6.

Pork Apple Pie

1 recipe pie pastry for 2 crusts
6 large, tart apples, peeled and chopped
¾ cup sugar
2 tablespoons all-purpose flour
¼ teaspoon salt
½ teaspoon cinnamon
¼ teaspoon nutmeg
⅔ cup salt pork, very finely diced (lean pork may be substituted; brown it first in butter)
2 teaspoons maple syrup
1 tablespoon butter, melted

Roll out half the dough to form a bottom crust and line a deep pie dish. Fill with the apples. In a medium-size bowl, mix the sugar, flour, salt, cinnamon, and nutmeg. Add the salt pork to the flour mixture; sprinkle evenly over the apples. Sprinkle the maple syrup over all. Roll out the remaining pastry; place over top. Pinch the edges of the pastry together; cut slits in the top to vent. Brush the top with the melted butter. Bake in a preheated 450°F oven for 10 minutes. Reduce the heat to 350°F and continue baking for 40-45 minutes. Serve warm with a slice of cheddar cheese, if desired. Serves 6.

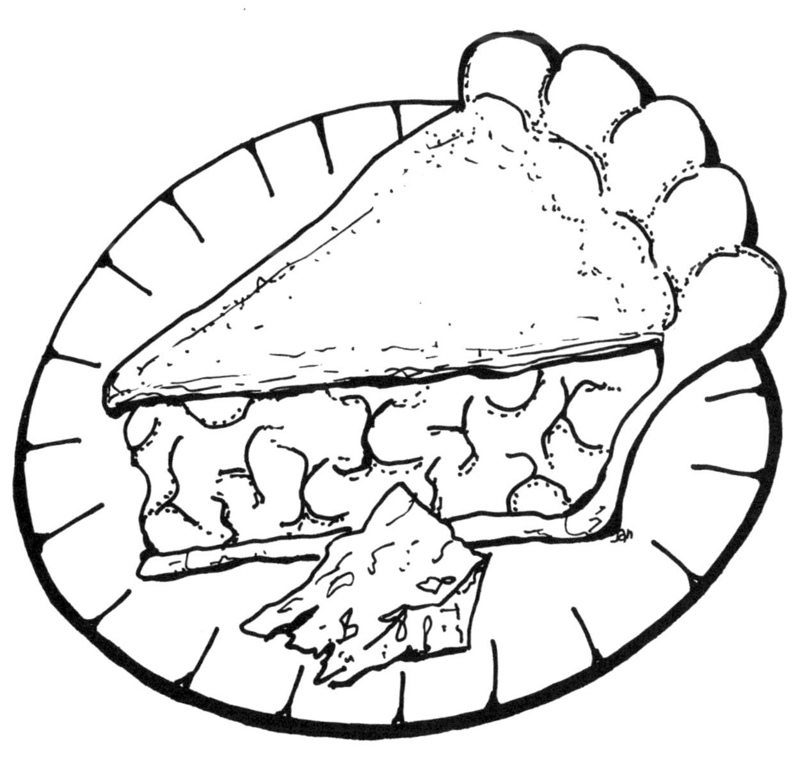

Boiled Cider Pie

1/3 cup boiled cider jelly
1/3 cup water
1 cup sugar
1/2 cup all-purpose flour
1/4 teaspoon nutmeg
1/4 teaspoon cinnamon
1 egg, beaten
1 tablespoon butter, softened
1/2 cup boiling water
1/4 cup chopped butternuts or walnuts
1 recipe pie pastry for 2 crusts

In a small saucepan, melt the cider jelly in 1/3 cup water over low heat. Stir slowly until it is a thick, dark red liquid. In a large bowl, combine the sugar, flour, nutmeg, and cinnamon. Add the butter, egg, boiled jelly, and boiling water; mix well. (The mixture will be very thin and soupy.) Add the nuts. Roll out half the dough to form a bottom crust and place in a 9-inch pie pan. Pour the filling into the pie shell. Cut the remaining pie pastry into 1 inch-wide strips and make a lattice top. Bake in a preheated 450°F oven for 10 minutes; reduce the heat to 350°F and continue baking for 30 minutes. Serves 6.

Boiled cider jelly is much more concentrated than the boiled cider of the past; but by melting it in water, the consistency of boiled cider can be regained.
Look for boiled cider jelly in gourmet food stores or in shops that carry Vermont products.

Green Tomato Mincemeat

Boiling water
3 pounds green tomatoes, chopped
3 pounds apples, peeled and chopped
2 ½ cups seeded raisins
1 cup chopped suet
8 cups brown sugar
2 teaspoons salt
1 cup cider vinegar
1 tablespoon cinnamon
1 teaspoon nutmeg
1 teaspoon ground cloves
Juice and grated rind of 1 orange

In a large saucepan, pour the boiling water over the tomatoes; drain. Repeat this process. Place the tomatoes in a large covered pot. Add the apples, raisins, suet, brown sugar, and salt; cook over medium heat for 30 minutes. Add the vinegar, cinnamon, nutmeg, cloves, and the orange juice and rind. Simmer slowly, stirring occasionally, until the mixture is thick, about 2 hours. When done, the mincemeat is ready for use as a filling for tarts and pies. Extra mincemeat can be stored by immediately pouring it into hot, sterilized pint canning jars. Leave a ½-inch headspace. Seal and process the jars in a boiling water bath or steam canner for 25 minutes. Makes about 12 pints.

Gingerbread

1½ teaspoons baking soda
1 cup sour cream
1 cup molasses
2 cups all-purpose flour
½ cup sugar
1½ teaspoons ginger
½ teaspoon cinnamon
1 egg, beaten
¼ cup shortening, melted

In a large bowl, dissolve the baking soda in the sour cream; add the molasses. In a separate large bowl, sift together the flour, sugar, ginger, and cinnamon; fold into the molasses and sour cream mixture. Add the egg and shortening; mix well. Pour into a greased 9-inch square cake pan. Bake in a preheated 375°F oven for 1 hour. Serves 6.

Maple Baked Apples

4 tart apples
¾ cup raisins
1½ cups maple syrup
1½ cups water
1 tablespoon butter

Peel and core the apples; place in a baking dish. Fill the cores with the raisins. Add the maple syrup, water, and butter to the dish. Bake in a preheated 375°F oven, turning and basting the apples occasionally, until the syrup is thick and the apples are tender, 45-50 minutes. Serve warm with a little of the syrup poured over each apple. Serves 4.

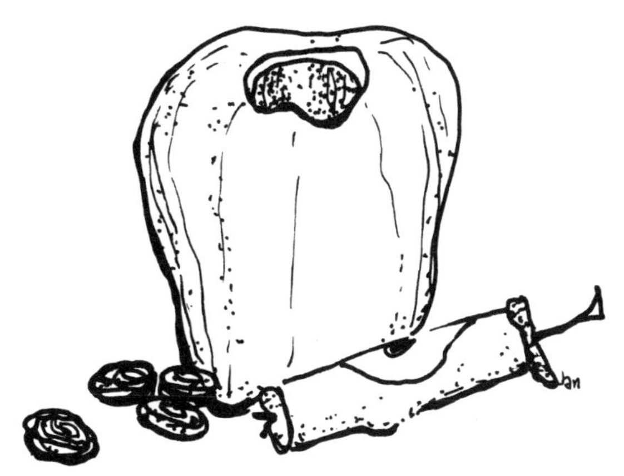

Maple Fudge

4 cups sugar
1 cup maple syrup
2 tablespoons corn syrup
$1\frac{1}{4}$ cups evaporated milk
4 tablespoons butter
2 cups mini marshmallows, packed tightly
$\frac{2}{3}$ cup chopped butternuts or walnuts

Bring the sugar, maple syrup, corn syrup, $\frac{1}{2}$ cup of the evaporated milk, and the butter to a boil over low to medium heat. Slowly add the remaining evaporated milk. Stir occasionally, and continue to boil slowly until a few drops of the mixture form a soft ball when dropped into cold water (about 15 minutes). Remove from the heat and allow to cool for 1 minute, then add the marshmallows and nuts. Stir rapidly until the marshmallows are melted and the mixture is very thick. Pour into a buttered 9-inch square pan. Cool completely and cut into squares.

Maple Molasses Cookies

1 cup sour cream
1 teaspoon baking soda
1 cup maple sugar
1 cup light molasses
2 eggs, beaten
½ teaspoon salt
1 teaspoon cinnamon
½ teaspoon nutmeg
½ teaspoon ground cloves
4½ cups all-purpose flour
¼ cup chopped butternuts or walnuts

In a large bowl, mix the sour cream and baking soda; add the maple sugar, molasses, and eggs. In a separate large bowl, sift together the salt, cinnamon, nutmeg, cloves, and flour; gradually stir into the molasses mixture. Add the nuts. Drop by the tablespoon onto greased cookie sheets. Bake in a preheated 375°F oven for 20 minutes. Remove the cookies to wire racks; cool. Makes 4-5 dozen cookies.

Maple Parfait

8 egg yolks
1 cup warm maple syrup
2 cups whipping cream
¼ teaspoon vanilla extract

In a small bowl, beat the egg yolks well. Mix with the maple syrup in the top of a double boiler. Cook the mixture slowly over medium heat, stirring frequently, until it reaches 170°F on a candy thermometer, or until the mixture coats a spoon when you lift it. Remove from the heat; cool. In a medium-size bowl, whip the cream until stiff. Add the cream and vanilla to to maple syrup mixture; mix well. Pour into a mold or parfait glasses; freeze for 3 hours before serving. Serves 4-6.

Hot Cheese Dip

4 ounces sharp cheddar cheese
1 cup mayonnaise
1 tablespoon Worcestershire sauce
$\frac{1}{8}$ teaspoon salt

Finely shred the cheese into a medium-size mixing bowl. Add the mayonnaise, Worcestershire sauce, and salt; mix thoroughly. Spoon into a 12-16-ounce baking dish. Bake, uncovered, in a preheated 350°F oven for 25 minutes. Serve hot with crackers.

Maple Doughnuts

2 eggs, beaten
1 cup sugar
4 tablespoons lard or shortening, melted
1 tablespoon baking powder
¾ cup whole milk
¾ cup maple syrup
½ teaspoon nutmeg
¼ teaspoon salt
4 cups all-purpose flour
2 pounds fat for frying (about 4 cups oil or shortening may be substituted)

In a large bowl, mix together the eggs, sugar, lard, baking powder, milk, maple syrup, nutmeg, and salt. Gradually add the flour to form a soft, manageable dough. Roll out on a lightly floured surface to about a ½-inch thickness. Cut into strips and twist into rings, or use a floured doughnut cutter. In a deep skillet, heat the fat to 370°F. Dip a spatula into the hot fat; use it to gently slide the doughnuts into the skillet. Fry 3 or 4 doughnuts at a time, being careful not to to crowd them in the skillet. When golden brown on both sides, remove carefully; drain on paper towels. Makes about 30 doughnuts.

Maple Salad Dressing

1/4 cup maple syrup
3 egg yolks, beaten
1 tablespoon lemon juice
1/4 cup vinegar
1/4 teaspoon paprika
1/4 teaspoon dry mustard
1/2 teaspoon salt
1/4 teaspoon pepper
1 cup cream

In a small saucepan, heat the maple syrup until it begins to boil; remove from the heat. Quickly stir in the egg yolks; heat again for 1 minute. Cool. Add the lemon juice, vinegar, paprika, mustard, salt, and pepper. Just before serving, whip the cream; fold into the mixture. Makes about 2 cups.